PUNCH AND JUDY

BY BILL SVANOE

★

★

DRAMATISTS
PLAY SERVICE
INC.

PUNCH AND JUDY was first presented by Century City Playhouse (Fara Marz Shahbazian, Artistic Director) in Los Angeles, California, in November 1995. It was directed by Joan Darling; the set design was by Linda Garen Smith; the lighting deisgn was by Scott Burkhardt and the stage manager was Mary K. Gabrysiak. The cast was as follows:

MARINA .... Janice Lynde
CAROL .... Joan Darling
MELODY .... Jessica Blodgett and Melissa Thompson

CAST

CAROL SPEARMAN

MARINA CLIFF

MELODY CHARM

TIME and PLACE

The action takes place at Marina Cliff's Park Avenue apartment and at a table of an uptown Madison Avenue bar. The time is the present.

PUNCH AND JUDY

ACT ONE

Scene 1

The lights come up on a small table that sits way downstage left. Carol Spearman sits in one chair and has her feet up on the other. She is dressed all in black as she talks on the phone. The only thing on the table is a drink which she stirs with her finger as she talks.

CAROL. I'd forgotten what New York is really like. I was walking up Lexington Avenue this morning when two large young men tried to borrow my purse. I offered to lend them my can of mace ... but they ran off halfway through the demonstration. Nobody has manners anymore. Don't worry about me, Joe. I can handle anything. I lived for two years in Los Angeles without a car or a lifestyle. I miss you terribly. Is there any chance you'll be coming to New York in the next few weeks? Your wife needs you? What for? Of course I'm jealous. She's the one with the husband the house and the kids. I'm the one with the ashtrays from two hundred hotels and the swizzle sticks from a thousand bars. *(Laughs.)*

I'm sorry, Joe. Sometimes I get a bit nostalgic. *(Laughs.)*

I'm sitting at our favorite New York table gathering strength. In ten minutes I have to go meet the richest divorced, lifted, peeled, liposucked, bimbo in America. She's hiring me to help her write a novel. It can't be her autobiography. Her divorce settlement from the blow-dried billionaire forbids it. She's created a new category all by herself, "nouveau disgusting." I have no idea why she chose me. Yes I *am* that desperate. I'm four months behind on my rent. My cat has been wandering up and down the hall interviewing possible new owners. Whenever I come in the door my parrot squawks at me, "co-dependent loser." I knew it was a bad idea to line the bottom of his cage with *New York* magazines.... I've never met this woman, but I can tell you exactly what her living room looks like.... First, she'll have one of those hideous pink and green ceramic dogs ... *(The curtain starts to rise slowly. The first thing visible is a hideous pink and green ceramic dog sitting on the stage staring out at the audience.)*

... that stares at you with an expression that says, "I just hid a dropping somewhere, and you'll never find it." She'll have matching off-white chairs, and sofa sitting on a Persian rug. *(The curtain continues to rise to reveal exactly the room Carol is describing.)*

The onyx end tables will have cut glass lamps on them that look like abused wood nymphs. The linen wallpaper will have taupe birds with green eyes. And the worst thing will be some kind of kinetic sculpture in the shape of ... *(Indeed there is a kinetic metal sculpture which is a representation of a man and a woman dressed in elegant dinner clothes. When the sculpture is "activated" it looks like the couple are walking hand in hand.)*

No ... cancel the kinetic sculpture, that's too much. I'm becoming a pathetic cynic.... The lady herself? She'll be wearing something sand and gold that costs more than most automobiles. *(Marina Cliff strolls into the room from R. She is wearing a beautiful sand-colored suit with a gold silk blouse and gold pumps. She carries a small tape recorder in one hand. She looks around the room, satisfied by it's beauty. We realize that she is the woman in the kinetic sculpture.)*

She'll be eager to tell me all her wonderful original ideas for the book. Like the one about the poor European beauty who's parents crushed her spirit as they groomed her to be a world champion.

MARINA. *(Into her tape recorder. She has an Hungarian accent.)* Suppose she was a poor European child whose parents crushed her spirit as.... No, She should be the daughter of a dictator who ...

CAROL. Or the daughter of a dictator ...
MARINA. Who escaped his clutches to become an international fashion ...
CAROL. Model, and then a wealthy Greek ...
MARINA. Tycoon, saw her walking down the ...
CAROL. Champs Elysee and taught her all about ...
MARINA. Finances and dirty dealings. He never made a pass at her until ...
CAROL. One day when they were alone on his island in ...
MARINA. The Adriatic and his passion ...
CAROL. Swept him away. She ran ...
MARINA. Screaming.... He asked forgiveness, but she never gave it until his ...
CAROL. Deathbed when she was as rich as he was. But of course he ...
MARINA. Left everything to her in the end, and she was finally able to find happiness with ...
CAROL. His chauffeur who was really his bastard son ... I know I'm too quick and too smart. Isn't that why you almost love me? Well, here I go. Into the valley of greed rode the Fortune Five Hundred. Just warming up. I'll call you tomorrow. Love you ... *(She hangs up and tosses off the rest of the drink. She stands up and walks offstage.*

Marina puts down her tape recorder. She is compulsively neat. She fluffs a few pillows and brushes unseen dust off things. The phone rings. Marina takes her time about answering it. Finally she picks a gold dolphin off the coffee table and talks into it.)

MARINA. Hello. BT ... I thought you were on your way to Amsterdam.... You can't find what?... Which jet are you in? ... Okay, look in the pocket of the third seat on the right. That's where you sat when we went to Kenya with Arnold. *(She straightens things out as she talks.)* It was there? I'm so glad ... I'm waiting to interview that writer.... Of course I'm still your friend. You know if it had been up to me, I would have taken only thirty million, but those silly lawyers.... I know you love to talk about money, but it upsets me. Don't worry BT, nobody's going to take advantage of me.... I know you love me, and I feel good about it. *(She puts the dolphin phone down* *and looks around the room. The doorbell chimes the first few bars of music such as "Lara's Theme"* from* Dr. Zhivago. *She goes to answer the door which is in the L. wall. She opens the door wide. There is nobody there. She turns away and is in the process of closing the door when Carol slips in the door and leans against the wall next to it. Marina turns back to see this person in black leaning against her wall. Carol finds herself staring right at the ceramic dog she so perfectly described. The two women regard each other.)*

CAROL. Hi.

MARINA. Hello. You are Carol?

CAROL. I am Carol I am.

MARINA. It's a pleasure to meet you.

CAROL. That feeling will go away soon. *(Marina holds out her hand to shake. They shake hands. Carol goes and walks around the kinetic sculpture. She can't believe her eyes.)*

MARINA. That's me and BT ...

CAROL. That was your pet name for him. BT ... "Big Thing."

MARINA. Yes. It still is my pet name for him. Somehow the press got hold of it a few years ago. Now that's all they call him.

CAROL. How did the press get hold of "it"?

MARINA. I don't know, servants overheard. It's impossible to keep things secret anymore.

CAROL. I don't have any trouble.

MARINA. Things are different when you're married to the seventy-fourth richest man in the world.

CAROL. I'm sure. You probably don't have to figure out which is the open end of those plastic bags at the supermarket fruit section.

MARINA. I haven't been in a fruit section in ten years. *(Carol regards the brass pineapple lamps.)*

CAROL. Not much has changed. It's still the same wonderful wacky place where truth and freshness battle mold and plastic for the souls of us all.

MARINA. My friend, Pookie Harkness, says writers have wonderful idiosyncrasies. How do you like to work?

* See Special Note on Songs and Recordings on copyright page.

CAROL. In a tub full of caviar.

MARINA. Oh, you're one of those witty people who are always saying clever things. This will be so amusing.

CAROL. My thought exactly. What was his pet name for you?

MARINA. I beg your pardon.

CAROL. You had a pet name for him; he must've had a pet name for you.

MARINA. *(Hesitates.)* I'm not a pet name sort of person.

CAROL. Me neither. However, in the sixth grade the boys would occasionally call me "tarantula twat."

MARINA. We won't be discussing personal things. Is that a problem for you?

CAROL. No problem here.

MARINA. *(Indicating the apartment.)* How do you like my place?

CAROL. Very restrained.

MARINA. I had some help, but the concept was all mine.

CAROL. *(Trying not to laugh as she looks around.)* It's certainly a unique statement. *(She moves the kinetic sculpture so the couple seems to be walking.)*

MARINA. BT gave me that for our eighth anniversary. It was to symbolize …

CAROL. The two of you walking hand in hand down the road of life together.

MARINA. Yes.

CAROL. How many more anniversaries were there before the union took the big bite and he ran off with the underwear model?

MARINA. Are you always this outspoken?

CAROL. I'm not being outspoken. If I told you the cheekbone implants were too much, that would be outspoken.

MARINA. Wouldn't that be rude?

CAROL. No, if I told you I hate people with ceramic dogs, that would be rude.

MARINA. Wouldn't that be the simple truth?

CAROL. If I told you I don't know what I'm doing here, that would be the truth.

MARINA. You're here because you need the money, so

wouldn't that be a lie?

CAROL. *(Realizes she has underestimated Marina. After a pause.)* It would.

MARINA. I'm not used to dealing with creative people. I hope you'll forgive an occasional misstep.

CAROL. I'm not used to dealing with impossibly wealthy people. I hope you'll forgive an occasional outburst of hysterical laughter. *(They regard each other.)*

MARINA. She wasn't an underwear model you know. The papers made such a fuss over the fact that she once posed in long johns for a mail-order catalogue.

CAROL. In this society you're known by your most basic act. If Mother Theresa had posed in long johns for LL Bean, she would be known as, "The Saint in the Skivvies." So are you friendly with her?

MARINA. I did meet Mother Theresa once. She's too small ... BT's current girlfriend's name is Melody Charm.

CAROL. Actually it's Myrna Chobnick. So are you friendly with her?

MARINA. We haven't met, but BT has flawless taste in women.

CAROL. It's all about taste isn't it? *(They regard each other.)*

MARINA. I was told you were acerbic and honest. I didn't want somebody who would pretend to be nice, and then stab me in the back later on. BT says with my kind of money I can't trust anybody.

CAROL. That's my situation as well.... How did you pick me?

MARINA. You were chosen by some of my people.

CAROL. There I was, Carol Spearman, tucked seductively between Salinger and Styron.

MARINA. I didn't burden myself with the details of the selection. It's not as if I were doing something important like changing hairstyles.

CAROL. I see.... What kind of a book do you want your name on?

MARINA. I want it to be exciting, uplifting, mysterious, timely, and a little sexy.

CAROL. You want people to thinks it's autobiographical, but

it isn't.

MARINA. That would be nice. I insist that it be a best seller.

CAROL. How many books are you prepared to buy?

MARINA. As many as it takes.

CAROL. I think the chances are good it will sell anyway.

MARINA. BT thinks it will sell very well. You stand to make a lot of money.

CAROL. And everybody will be happy. If you like, I'll just go write the book. You don't have to do any work.

MARINA. I want to do the work.... My friend, Pooky Harkness, says the greatest pleasure comes from creating something.

CAROL. Pooky sounds alarmingly fascinating.

MARINA. I should warn you, I'm very sensitive to being mocked.

CAROL. Sorry. I'm alone so much, I don't realize how I sound.

MARINA. I know exactly how I sound all the time. I turn on the TV and there I am being quoted or interviewed. Just last night, after a sublime dinner at Mort's with Calvin and Kelly, I was crossing the street and there printed on the side of a newspaper truck was, "Marina warns new bimbo about BT's strange habits."

CAROL. Is there any truth to any of it?

MARINA. *(Smiles.)* I've been interviewed by the best in the world. Nobody's ever gotten a word from me that I didn't want them to.

CAROL. Not me. I never know what's going to come flying out of my mouth, like bats fleeing a damp neurotic cave.

MARINA. Were the terms of our arrangement explained to you?

CAROL. You get sole credit, I get all the royalties. I'm never to tell a soul that I wrote a word of the book. I'm also never to talk or write about you to anybody, or I forfeit all royalties and can be sued for damages.

MARINA. Are you comfortable with that?

CAROL. Yes. It must be terrible to be so suspicious of everybody.

MARINA. *(Sharply.)* Nobody feels sorry for somebody with fifty million dollars. *(She regrets having let her guard down for an instant.)* The purpose of this meeting was to determine if we can work together. I also want you to be comfortable with me.

CAROL. I'm very comfortable.

MARINA. Do you think we could be friends?

CAROL. *(Hesitates.)* Not a chance in the world.

MARINA. Good. I was so afraid you were going to pretend to be sincere.

CAROL. Your fears are superfluous.

MARINA. Your faux honesty seems alarmingly real.

CAROL. I like your simulated stoic isolation. It has classic simplicity.

MARINA. Would you excuse me for a moment. I have to give my secretary a few details before she goes out.

CAROL. Sure. *(Marina exits. Carol immediately goes and picks up the gold dolphin phone. She dials impatiently.)* Steve, it's Carol. I can't do this thing with the fifty-mill monster. Get me something easy like six months as a combination cook and whore on a Liberian prison ship.... Help!... *(She hangs up quickly and smiles pleasantly as Marina walks back in.)* I hope you don't mind. I was just calling the hospital to check on my mother.

MARINA. Your mother's in the hospital? What does she have?

CAROL. It's more what she doesn't have. She doesn't have a memory or a bladder. *(Marina stares at Carol as Carol puts the dolphin phone back on the coffee table.)*

MARINA. About the book; I once met a woman who was the daughter of a dictator. She ran away and became a fashion model. A Greek Tycoon befriended her and ... *(She looks at Carol smiling.)* It's cliché isn't it?

CAROL. Numbingly.

MARINA. That's why I need you. I don't want to be laughed at.

CAROL. I understand. Tell me your favorite story.

MARINA. *(Impatient.)* My favorite story is my own.... I can't use it.

CAROL. Maybe you can. Tell me your story.

MARINA. I'm not going to tell you anything that hasn't been in a thousand newspapers.
CAROL. I don't care where it's been.
MARINA. *(After a moment.)* As I'm sure you know, I'm Swiss. My father was German, my mother was Hungarian. I spent most of the first sixteen years of my life working to be an Olympic figure skater. At the European championships my closest rival missed a practice jump and fell into me. She cut my knee ligament with the blade of her skate. I could never skate at world class level after that.
CAROL. Did it hurt?
MARINA. I never had a moments pain in my knee. Two years later at a charity event in Geneva, I met BT. He was just a cute young man in business school with no money. We fell in love and got married. BT got this job scouting real estate for that rich Australian, Colin Shields, and for a year we traveled all over the world in private jets and stayed in the best places. It was a wonderful time. Colin disappeared over the South Atlantic and suddenly BT was without a job. After living like royalty, we didn't have a penny. We came to New York. BT got his real estate broker's license and I worked as his secretary. Twenty years later, he was worth two billion ...
CAROL. That year traveling around in the jet. What a time you must've had.
MARINA. It was like a dream ... Every once in awhile, I wake up in the morning and think I'm in the Loire valley with Richie. He's gone to get our coffee and he'll be back any minute ... *(She stops. This is not territory she wants to get into.)* Why are we talking about this? We can't do anything about our real story.
CAROL. You could do a story about a young couple who get used to thinking they have everything, and then one day have nothing ... *(Marina looks at Carol for a moment, lost in memories.)*
MARINA. Maybe ...
CAROL. Terrific. Let's get to work.... First you tell me what it was like. I'll organize it into some kind of outline and once we have that we can ...

MARINA. *(Coldly.)* You don't have the job yet. *(She smiles at Carol who is brought up short.)*

CAROL. *(Embarrassed.)* Oh ... of course not. I was just proposing a way to work on ... the book ... *(Marina behaves as if she were interviewing a prospective servant. She walks around Carol. Marina picks up the gold phone as if she expected to find Carol stole something from it.)*

MARINA. BT says that there are only four reasons people do anything; lust, love, revenge and money. He says never work with somebody until you know which reason applies.

CAROL. Is that what he says?... *(She reaches down and takes off her shoes. She holds them out to Marina who gingerly takes them and looks them over. She holds them up so light shines through the holes in the soles. She hands the shoes back to Carol. Marina looks down at Carol's feet.)*

MARINA. You have holes in your shoes and in your stockings.

CAROL. Have your people call my "people" when you make your decision. If it happens that we don't work together, maybe we'll run into each other on the Orient Express. We can vie for the favors of a mad Polish nobleman and play whist through the restless spicy night ... *(She turns with a lithe spin and exits out the front door. Marina stands there for a long moment. Carol comes out D. and sits down at her table as the lights come up on it. She picks up the phone and talks into it.)* She may be the most unpleasant person I ever met. She hated me, but she'll hire me ... *(Marina has picked up the gold phone and is talking into it.)*

MARINA. *(On phone.)* Pookie, darling, she's the most unpleasant person I've ever met.... As you remember I have met both Castro and Kaddafi ...

CAROL. *(On phone.)* I was just the right combination of eccentric and acerbic ...

MARINA. *(On phone.)* But if she writes the way she talks, people will think I'm smart. She's not scared of me, which I like.

CAROL. *(On phone.)* I have to tell you, Steve. this woman scares me to death. *(Marina presses a button on the bottom of the phone and we hear a tape recorder play.)*

CAROL'S VOICE. *(On tape.)* Steve, it's Carol. I can't do this thing with the fifty-mill monster. Get me something easy like six months as a combination cook and whore on a Liberian prison ship ... Help!... *(Marina stops the tape recorder and says into the phone.)*

MARINA. *(On phone.)* I so pity people who don't have control. *(The lights and curtain come down.)*

END OF SCENE 1

Scene 2

The lights come up on Carol's table. Carol is on the phone and is stirring her drink with her finger.

CAROL. *(Laughing.)* No I hadn't heard that one.... Did you know the entire life span of the Brazilian Buzz Fly is twenty-four hours? *(Laughs.)* Right, what do you do if you've only got one day? Do you pick up the cleaning?... Now there's a situation where having your pizza delivered in under thirty minutes really means something. *(Laughs.)* I don't like the sound of that cough. Are you smoking again?... Damnit, Joe, you promised.... Of course your wife never yells at you, she has the brains of a bicycle pump ... I know she has a great body ... *(She holds the phone by her side and screams silently in rage. Then she calmly brings the phone back to her ear.)* I could have a great body too if I'd had an affair with a plastic surgeon like she did. No I'm not trying to emasculate you, I'm trying to eviscerate you.... Yeah, I have to go too. Another fun day with the Swiss bitch. Love you ... *(She walks offstage as the lights on her table dim. The lights come up full on Marina's apartment. Marina is on the dolphin phone. She is wearing a beautiful, expensive outfit as well as extensive jewelry.)*

MARINA. *(Giggles.)* BT, that's the most sexist joke I ever heard.... You are terrible.... Ach poo!... *(Pauses.)* I miss you too darling.... Did you get your flu shot?... You didn't but *she* got hers?... *(She holds the phone by her side and screams silently in rage. She puts the phone back to her ear and says calmly.)* I'm fine, I just noticed some lint on the couch.... I'm having a wonderful time working on my book with this Carol person. She's a nasty little worm, but smart as can be.... Of course she's not as smart as you.... Love you, sweetie.... Talk to you soon. *(She hangs up. She picks up her leather appointment book and goes to the bookcase with her back to the door. The doorbell chimes the first few bars of music such as "Lara's Theme"* from* Dr. Zhivago.*)* Come in. *(Carol walks in. She is carrying a small pharmacy paper bag. Marina starts talking right away as if Carol were her secretary.)* What should we do about the guest list on the island this weekend? The Walkers are battling the Sterns again.

CAROL. Shoot the Walkers. Hang the Sterns.

MARINA. Oh, Carol. I thought you were my secretary.

CAROL. And I thought you were my mother.

MARINA. Don't you find that people tire of your smart mouth after awhile?

CAROL. No, I find they tire of it right away.

MARINA. Did you pick up my prescriptions? *(Carol silently holds out the drugstore paper bag. Marina takes the bag and puts it on the coffee table. Dismissively.)* Thank you, darling.... You know you're five minutes late. I only have forty-five minutes today.

CAROL. Well, then let's have at it. *(She goes and sits down in a chair. She takes out a bunch of typed pages.)* I have the new outline all typed up. We have a good story here.

MARINA. I've been thinking; my lead character whines too much.

CAROL. Yesterday you liked whining.

MARINA. And I think the whole thing about her being a sled dog trainer from Iceland is too cliché.

CAROL. Too cliché?... Yesterday, you thought it was magical. Are you aware that this is the eighth outline I've typed up?

* See Special Note on Songs and Recordings on copyright page.

MARINA. Isn't that your job? I'm paying you a lot of money for you to sit there until we work out whatever I want. *(She jots a note in her appointment book. During this scene she always seems to be busy making notes in her appointment book and fussing with things in her apartment. She tends to act as if Carol were this annoyance she is putting up with.)*

CAROL. I can't give you what you want.

MARINA. And what is that?

CAROL. You want BT back in your bed.

MARINA. I had him in my bed last week..

CAROL. Really?... Tell me about that?

MARINA. He misses certain little things I ... *(She stops angrily and smiles coldly.)* Very clever, MS Spearman. You thought you had me didn't you?

CAROL. You almost spilled your guts. Everyone thinks BT is only breathing fire on the flanks of fair Melody Charm.

MARINA. I told you; nobody gets anything out of me ... ever!... Please don't test my patience like a new chambermaid putting the sheets on sideways.

CAROL. Let's get on with it. Enough girlish banter.

MARINA. I had the most wonderful idea in the shower this morning. Suppose our heroine steps off the train at Grand Central and is knocked flat by a commuter. She wakes up in a hospital and can't remember who she is. She gets a job as a nurse and starts having a hot affair with an older doctor. Then she is hit on the head by a tray of appetizers at the Tea Room and she remembers, the doctor is her father ... *(She stares at Carol.)* Why aren't you taking notes on this?

CAROL. I was mesmerized.

MARINA. Carol, this is a great story I thought up.

CAROL. It certainly is. It's also the plot of Jackie Craven's new best seller.

MARINA. It is? *(Embarrassed.)* Are you sure? I'll kill Pookie.

CAROL. That's probably a culturally sound decision.

MARINA. Do you have to be so savagely critical all the time? Let's move along; I'm running out of time.

CAROL. I'm out of stories.

MARINA. You can't be.

CAROL. I am. Sometimes you call the market for pork chops and they're out.

MARINA. *(Threatening.)* If my market told me they were out of pork chops, I'd stop shopping there.

CAROL. What's wrong with any one of the twelve other stories I came up with in the last month? They had drama, structure, tension ...

MARINA. They weren't me.

CAROL. Excuse me?...

MARINA. They didn't have élan, style, sparkle.

CAROL. Writing a novel isn't like redecorating a bedroom.

MARINA. Thank god. I'm never going through that again. *(The phone rings. She answers it quickly.)* Hello ... *(She answers in an elegant low tone. When she realizes who it is, her voice changes to more like a schoolgirl.)* BT, I didn't expect to hear from you until Monday.... Of course you know I'd do anything for you ... *(There is a long pause. She is upset, but she tries not to show it.)* My writer is here. Can I call you back in a teeny bit?... Oh, you're in the helicopter.... I know it sounds very simple, but don't I have to check with Harold and Bob?... Well, if it's only for one day.... Let me think about it for a few minutes ... *(Testy.)* I said let me think about it ... just a few minutes.... Bye love ... *(She hangs up the phone. She is quite distressed, but she pretends nothing is going on. Carol is watching her like a hawk.)* You can't be out of stories.

CAROL. Okay, how about this.... There's this very bright twenty-year old, from a poor Boston family who comes to New York. Her life's desire is to write witty insightful articles for The New Yorker. Her first night in New York, she meets a daytime talk show host in a bar. They go to bed and it is wonderful. The next day he hires her to be a talent booker on his show. At lunch time they make it in his office. That night, she finds out from the producer of the show that he is married with four kids. She's crazy about him so they keep having "lunches." He never says he's going to leave his wife. She gets to know his kids and his wife. She likes them all. She saves one daughter from suicide and helps another get into Sarah Lawrence. He has to fire her, because people are getting suspicious. She follows him back and forth from coast to coast getting whatever job she can to be near him. Before she knows it, twenty years have gone by and she's no closer to having an article published in *The New Yorker* ...

MARINA. Why does she stay with him through all that?

CAROL. He makes her laugh. He gets her jokes, and the sex is outstanding.

MARINA. There must be more.

CAROL. He's one of the few men who isn't afraid of her.

MARINA. *(After a moment.)* How does it end?

CAROL. His wife dies suddenly. She marries him, and they live happily ever after.

MARINA. Does she ever get an article published in *The New Yorker?*

CAROL. No.... There has to be some irony.

MARINA. I don't believe the ending ...

CAROL. Why not?

MARINA. It doesn't ring true ... I have to cut our session a bit short today. Think about that ending. I like the beginning.

CAROL. I like the ending.

MARINA. Does she have to be from Boston?

CAROL. Yes.

MARINA. Why?

CAROL. Where would you like her to be from?

MARINA. Iceland.

CAROL. What is it you like about Iceland? I have never known anybody fictional or real who came from Iceland.

MARINA. We refueled our small jet there one night a few years ago. BT and I went for a walk by this river that ran with boiling water. Puffs of steam rose up from it and drifted over us like clouds. One minute we would be in full view of the airport and the city, the next instant we would be lost in this dense cloud. The cloud would pass over in a few seconds, but for those precious moments, BT and I were completely alone and together.

CAROL. That's beautiful. It's a magical powerful image.

MARINA. You don't have to say that; I'm paying you anyway.

CAROL. I know you're paying me anyway. All I said was, your description of you and BT at the Iceland airport was beautiful. What's the problem?

MARINA. I don't know if you mean it or not.

CAROL. What do you care if I mean it or not? Go out this afternoon and buy a country or something.

MARINA. See, that's why I can't talk to anybody about anything. They take it and twist it into whatever they want.

CAROL. Wait a minute, Queen Marina. I gave you a compliment. That's what just happened. I don't give compliments if I don't mean them.

MARINA. How do I know that? How do I know you're not trying to become my best friend, so you can travel with me, get invited to my chalet or my villa, travel by private jet, eat and drink for free ...

CAROL. *(Pauses.)* I guess you don't know. *(The phone rings. Marina picks it up.)*

MARINA. Hello ... BT ... I'm still meeting with my writer. I said I'd call you back sweetie. Five minutes ... *(She hangs up the phone and stares at her couch.)*

CAROL. Don't lend him any of your money.

MARINA. What?

CAROL. BT asked you to lend him some money for a day ...

MARINA. How did you know?... *(She stops and lies defensively.)* That wasn't what he asked.... Do you expect me to take financial advice from a broke, starving, moderately talented writer?

CAROL. That wasn't financial advice; it was personal advice.

MARINA. And why would I take personal advice from a stupid woman who's never married and has no friends because of her twenty-year infatuation with a married talk show host who's never going to leave his wife. *(Carol stares angrily at Marina.)*

CAROL. How did you know?

MARINA. BT had people check you out.

CAROL. *(Evenly.)* What fun we're all having.

MARINA. I like your story; the writer and the talk show host.

Write up an outline and let's look at it.

CAROL. No.

MARINA. I beg your pardon.

CAROL. I said, "no." That's my story; you can't have it.

MARINA. Of course I can have it; read your contract. Any story you tell me, I can use. *(Carol stares angrily at Marina.)*

CAROL. Prove I told it to you. *(Marina picks a silver sculpture of a wolf off the table. She presses some buttons on the bottom. From speakers in the wall comes Carol's voice saying.)*

CAROL'S VOICE. Prove I told it to you. *(Marina presses buttons on the wolf and sets it down.)*

MARINA. BT put that in place when he used to have meetings here. I'm so happy I forgot to have it taken out when he left. *(Carol stares angrily at Marina.)* So I will expect you to write up your story with a more "realistic" ending.

CAROL. You arrogant, spoiled, stupid twit!... You're afraid of everybody and everything. I put up with your idiotic ideas and your using me as a delivery boy for your prescriptions and repaired shoes because I don't want to be on the street. But you can't have my story. I won't write it, and you can't make me.

MARINA. You don't want to cross me and BT. We can make it impossible for you to get a job anywhere in the Western Hemisphere. We can have you killed if we like.

CAROL. BT can do all that. You can't do a thing. You can't stand not being Mrs Richard Cliff anymore. You're a joke and an embarrassment. Everybody in the world feels sorry for you.

MARINA. Nobody feels sorry for somebody with fifty-million dollars.

CAROL. Least of all me. You can stay here alone until you go crazy and claw that sickening paper off the walls. You're the saddest person I've ever met.

MARINA. You're pathetic. You never had the talent to get an article in *The New Yorker.* Joe probably never married you because you were a lousy....

CAROL. Don't you dare say that. I'm the best he's ever had.

MARINA. Do you know why you were selected?... I asked for a mediocre hack writer who could only write trash. You were hired because you're not that good.

CAROL. *(Very angry.)* The same reason BT dumped you.

MARINA. No, that's the reason Joe never married you. Did somebody say you were smart? You're the bimbo here. *(Carol reaches out and slaps Marina on the face. Marina slaps her right back, and with a quick martial arts flip, Carol finds herself flat on the couch with Marina standing over her.)* I know how to take care of myself. All you know is how to be clever.... You're fired. *(Marina stalks out of the room through the R. door which leads to her bedroom. After a moment, Carol gets up. She walks out the front door, closing it quietly behind her.)*

END OF SCENE 2

Scene 3

The lights come up on Carol's table. She is talking on the phone and stirring her drink with a finger.

CAROL. I'm the only one who tells you the truth.... You know what tomorrow is don't you?... Her birthday.... You got her a nightgown last year. Have your secretary pick up a dress at Bergdog's. She's a size six damnit ... *(Laughs.)* No, Patricia, your wife is a size six. Your secretary is a size fourteen if the moon is favorable.... When did you get a new secretary?... How come you know her size?... *(Carol takes the phone away from her ear and screams silently. She puts the phone back to her ear and speaks calmly.)* When will I see you next?... You're taking her to Hawaii again? Didn't you just go there?... Two years ago? Has it been that long since her last suicide attempt?.. I am being civilized. Haven't I been "civilized" the last twenty years?... No I don't have separation anxiety. I have stupidity anxiety. *(Becomes cool and detached.)* Of course I want you to have a good time. Yes, I have to go too ... *(Dryly.)* Send me a postcard of a volcano. *(She hangs up the phone. She sits there for a moment. She licks some liquor off her fingers. She gets up and ex-*

its L. The lights come up on Marina's apartment. She is beautifully dressed in a skirt suit. She talks on the gold dolphin phone as she examines the wallpaper.)

MARINA. I'm not going to Le Cirque with the girls. We're trying a different place. Linda's ex has been sitting at the next table with his current, and it's much too tabloid ... BT, I hesitate to mention this, but I'm just a teeny bit worried about.... I know what you said, but it's been six days not one.... Okay, I won't worry ... I told you, I'm paying her off. I'm going to write the book myself. I've been reading a lot; it doesn't look that difficult ... *(Laughs.)* Don't be mean.... Remember it was me who told you to buy the Main Street Hotel all those years ago. No it wasn't your mother ... *(She holds the phone by her side and screams silently. She puts the phone back to her ear and says calmly.)* Okay, sure. I have to go too. Love and kisses ... *(She hangs up the phone. She picks up the tape recorder and talks into it.)* Chapter Three. Kimberly danced down the marble steps. She loved those steps. Someday she would have her own marble steps. She thought about seeing him again. Maybe today would be the day. She looked down at the ketchup-spattered waitress uniform and thought ... *(She angrily throws the tape recorder at the couch. She sits down in a chair and stares at the wall.)* Stupid, stupid ... *(After a moment, there is a knock at the front door.)* Come in. *(Carol walks in and looks around.)*

CAROL. I came for my check.

MARINA. It was sent to your apartment.

CAROL. *(Angry.)* I told you, I wanted to pick it up.

MARINA. I didn't get the message.

CAROL. Well, cancel that check and write me a new one on the spot.

MARINA. Don't be silly.

CAROL. I don't trust the mails. My contract states that I will receive all checks in person.

MARINA. It wasn't sent by mail. It was sent by bonded messenger.

CAROL. I don't care if it was sent by Henry Kissinger.

MARINA. He's out of town. I spoke to his wife this ...

CAROL. Stop it!... I want my check right now. It's a matter

of contract.

MARINA. You had wanted a certified check. If I write you a check, it won't be certified.

CAROL. Your bank is right on the corner. I'm sure when you call they barbecue a teller if that's what you want. Just call, and they'll have a replacement check here in five minutes. *(Marina glares at Carol. Marina picks up her phone and punches one number. The phone automatically sends out seven tones.)*

MARINA. *(Into phone.)* Les, dear, it's Marina. There was some kind of silly mix-up on that check to Carol Spearman. Would you be a dear and send another one up here right away? Thanks so much ... *(She hangs up the phone and regards Carol.)* I wasn't aware that if I fired you, you got paid anyway.

CAROL. Really?

MARINA. I can't believe your lawyers were better than my lawyers. *(Carol walks over and puts the kinetic sculpture in motion.)*

CAROL. What lawyers? I wrote my own contract. So how's the book going?

MARINA. *(Trying to hide her rage.)* Wonderful. I'm almost finished.

CAROL. That's great. What story did you decide on?

MARINA. Something completely different.

CAROL. You mean something about a young dancer from Nebraska who comes to New York and gets involved with a music reviewer who's married to the daughter of the owner of the paper? Her name would be Candice or Kimberly.

MARINA. You're just so smart aren't you? *(There is a long pause. Carol swings the figure of Marina on the sculpture.)*

CAROL. Did he pay you back?

MARINA. What makes you so sure I lent him anything?

CAROL. You did, didn't you?

MARINA. Impossible foul woman. *(Pause.)*

CAROL. You're having a tough time with the book aren't you?

MARINA. Hardly. It's flowing like champagne. *(They stare at each other.)*

CAROL. Let me help you with it. I can't afford to give back the money, but I don't feel right taking it and not doing the work.

MARINA. You did the work. You sat here every day for a month. You made twelve outlines. You delivered my prescriptions, my shoes and sometimes even my cleaning.

CAROL. I was heroic.... If you're worried about being taken advantage of, I'll sign a paper agreeing never to visit your villa, fly in your plane, sail on your yacht or be your friend.

MARINA. That won't be necessary.

CAROL. Are you sure? Sometimes friendship can sneak up you. There you are stuck for life with this *person.*

MARINA. Nothing sneaks up on me.

CAROL. Too bad; that can be fun sometimes. Show me what you've got.

MARINA. You won't like it.

CAROL. You haven't written a word, have you?

MARINA. I know any day it will come pouring out.

CAROL. Better carry a mop.

MARINA. I like you, Carol.

CAROL. What?

MARINA. I like you.

CAROL. *(Wary.)* Are we on TV? Is one of your medications wearing off?

MARINA. I don't know if I have any real friends. BT is the only person I can trust.

CAROL. Isn't this the same guy who was photographed unzipping sweet Melody Charm in a public elevator?

MARINA. They got stuck between floors.

CAROL. Is that where they got stuck?

MARINA. If I don't trust him, that means I have nobody I can trust.

CAROL. I don't trust anybody.

MARINA. You don't trust Joe?

CAROL. I love him, I'd die for him, but I don't trust him. Why do you like me?

MARINA. You come close to telling me the truth.

CAROL. I'm impressed. Most people think I am telling the truth. What's going on?

MARINA. I'm so bored with everything. When I was a kid, I looked forward so much to every day. Now, I can't wait for the days to be over.

CAROL. How can you be bored? You can afford to do anything.

MARINA. I've been everywhere. I've done everything.

CAROL. Everything is boring?... I don't want to hear that. I'm only holding this life together because I want to see Michalengelo's David and I want them to invent French fries with no fat ...

MARINA. The David is just a statue. Get a grip on reality.

CAROL. Reality is a one-room apartment that's never the right temperature and vibrates like a teacup on a lawnmower every ten minutes when the subway goes under. Reality is dinner with my cat who has a more interesting social life than I do. Reality is I'm too old and too smart ever to have any real friends ... I have a death-grip on reality, and it's not working.

MARINA. You think my life is such a wonderful simple existence don't you? Everything is taken care of for me, so I just float on a blissful cloud. It's not that simple. The money doesn't mean what you think it does.

CAROL. What does it have to mean? What the hell do you want?

MARINA. I want secrets, whispers, quick caresses in hallways. I want somebody to sneak a look at me and wonder what it would be like to press me against a wall. I want to look forward to a furtive meeting at a small café down a winding narrow street.... I want to sit on a dock and dangle my feet in the water while I wait for his reflection to appear over my shoulder. *(She smiles at Carol.)*

CAROL. I understand: no matter how much money I had, Joe wouldn't marry me.

MARINA. Think about my situation. I can't "date" anyone. There's only a few men in the world who wouldn't either be intimidated by or after my money.

CAROL. Are you secretly hoping BT will come back to you?

MARINA. Of course.

CAROL. You'd forgive him for all the humiliation and pain

he put you through?

MARINA. In an instant, and it's not just because I like being Mrs. Richard Cliff.... However you were right about that; I loved being Mrs. Richard Cliff.... Wouldn't you forgive Joe if he agreed to marry you?

CAROL. I don't know. I'm so angry at him right now. He wanted me to pick up a birthday present for his wife. He doesn't even know when my birthday is.

MARINA. Haven't you done that for him before?

CAROL. Just because one agrees to lift their skirt on the floor of the Carlyle coatroom one long ago night doesn't mean one will automatically do it again. One should be asked nicely every time.

MARINA. I know, but "one" can't say in the moment of passion, "hey buster this is a one ride ticket you have here." *(Carol laughs heartily. Marina enjoys that she made Carol laugh. Marina chuckles a bit herself.)*

CAROL. You can be very funny.

MARINA. When I was skating, at the end of the day I'd be so tired I couldn't see. My legs burned, my hips ached, but I would feel so alive.... Three of us girls would go across the street to Herman's strudel shop. We'd sit at a window table and I would make comments about the people walking by. I always had the girls laughing so hard they cried. I went to the coffee shop the first day after my ligament healed. The girls were so glad to see me, and expressed "concern," but I was no longer part of that group. I was just another person walking by the window. I haven't belonged anywhere since ...

CAROL. That must feel terrible.

MARINA. Nobody ever knows what I really feel.

CAROL. Including BT? *(Marina doesn't answer.)* When did it start going wrong for you and BT?

MARINA. He likes all his things to be new and shiny, and in perfect working order at all times.

CAROL. His "things"?

MARINA. Don't bother, Carol. The feminist manifesto never would stick to my door.

CAROL. *(Laughs.)* I wouldn't touch that with a ten foot polemic. *(After a pause.)* How was it when he visited your bed last week?

MARINA. Fantastic.... We both love brief, dangerous encounters.

CAROL. You told me some of your real feelings. How come? You said I'd never get anything out of you.

MARINA. I was mistaken. Everybody is mistaken now and then.

CAROL. I only remember anger from my childhood My father was angry because he got sick. Then my mother was angry when she was left with no help and no insurance. My mother would ask me a question about something, and when I would start to answer, she would walk away as if I didn't exist. So I learned to pretend to be there with her. I pretended we were a happy family, but I knew I was alone.

MARINA. So then you understand how I feel?

CAROL. I understand. My mother never taught me a thing. She didn't teach me how to wash myself. She didn't teach me how to get dressed or how to do my hair. Nobody taught me how to have a friend, how to kiss a boy ... *(She fights back tears.)*

MARINA. Carol ...

CAROL. I want to be present in this world before I die. I want to trust somebody without question. Do you know if you really have a true friend? What's the test?

MARINA. I don't know. *(There is a knock at the door. An envelope slips through the slot in the door and drops silently on the stage by the door.)* Your certified check. *(She goes over and picks up the envelope and hands it to Carol.)*

CAROL. A hundred thousand dollars. Do you have any idea what this means to me? I can fall asleep at night for the first time in two years. I can buy a coffee maker that has all it's parts. I can get a new pair of glasses ... *(Marina is walking around adjusting things on her coffee table as Carol talks.)* Did you hear what I said?

MARINA. Something about coffee.

CAROL. You weren't listening.

MARINA. Was I supposed to? Are you under the impression that you are something other than an employee?

CAROL. Yes, I thought.... You told me intimate details that you've never told anyone else.

MARINA. Yes, I did.

CAROL. We were sharing things that ...

MARINA. I guess we were.

CAROL. Then why?... *(She goes cold as stone. The rage builds in her.)* My contract.... Anything you tell me, I can't repeat to anybody or I get sued.... You realized you could tell me anything.... It wasn't a matter of friendship or trust ...

MARINA. It's a matter of contract ...

CAROL. You miserable, miserable bitch. Why did you do that to me?

MARINA. You did it to me first. Maybe now you have some idea what it's like to be me.

CAROL. I will never have any idea what it's like to be heartless, and without feeling.

MARINA. Oh don't be so hurt. You're tougher than that. You can't tell me you were really talking to me.

CAROL. *(Hesitates.)* Right. I thought I had you fooled.

MARINA. I'm never fooled. I'm out of time for today. Ten sharp tomorrow?

CAROL. I'll be here. *(Aside.)* You impossible silicone slut.

MARINA. I'm tired of your grotesque innuendo. They're *saline* not silicone. *(Carol puts the check in her pocket and starts for the door. The phone rings. Marina picks it up.)* Hello ... *(To Carol.)* It's for you.

CAROL. *(Scared.)* For me?... It can't be for me.

MARINA. It's for you ... *(Carol goes gingerly and takes the phone.)*

CAROL. Hello.... *(As soon as she hears the voice on the phone, her whole body goes limp and she starts shaking. She tries to maintain a calm voice.)* Yes, Patricia, I recognize your voice ... I know there's only one reason you would call me ... *(She listens.)* I understand. Thank you for calling ... *(She hangs up the phone. She carefully places it on the couch. She starts for the door in a daze.)*

MARINA. Joe died, didn't he?

CAROL. *(Turns, vicious.)* How did you know. How did you know?

MARINA. *(Snaps.)* I'm not as stupid as you think.

CAROL. Yes, he died. His wife called to tell me. She also told me she's known about our affair all these years. She doesn't want to see me at the funeral or the memorial service ... I thought she was my friend. *(She starts again for the door. The phone rings. Marina picks it up.)*

MARINA. Hello.... BT.... Okay, check in the little closet in the bathroom; your coat should be there. *(She stiffens.)* What?... What are you telling me Richie?... *(She sits down on the couch. Her tone makes Carol stop and turn around.)* You told me it would only be for one day. But it's my money, not yours. I know I cosigned but ... Richie, that's my money. I don't have anything else.... What does that mean? *(Screams.)* You can't be broke. BT, this is a joke isn't it?... No you won't call me tomorrow you'll keep talking to me now. You ... *(He has hung up. Marina puts the phone down carefully. She looks over at Carol.)* BT says he's broke. I had cosigned his loan, so the bank took my fifty million. All of it..

CAROL. Easy come, easy go.

MARINA. This is not funny you broken-down brown recluse spider bitch.

CAROL. What else could it possibly be?

MARINA. But I'm broke!... I don't have anything!... Don't you understand?...

CAROL. *(Deadly calm.)* I understand wonderfully. Have a nice day ... *(She exits. She closes the door quietly behind her. Marina sits in shock as the curtain comes down.)*

END OF ACT ONE

ACT TWO

Scene 1

Carol is sitting at her downstage table with the phone on it. She is stirring a drink with her finger. Also on the table is two inch thick manila envelope. After a moment, Carol punches up a number on the phone without picking up the handset. Then she picks up her drink and drains it in one gulp. The lights go down on Carol's table and come up on Marina's apartment. Marina is sitting on the couch in an old gray sweat suit. She is surrounded by cardboard moving boxes. On the coffee table are stacks and stacks of papers, file folders and photo albums. Marina picks a magazine article out of a file folder and begins to read it. The phone rings. She picks it up quickly.

MARINA. BT?... Of course it's me. I don't have to be out until the end of the week. I don't know where I'm going. Bob and Sissy invited me to tour on their yacht for a month, but I don't feel like seeing those people. You know how that Euro-trash tends to pile up in one place.... No, I'm not mad at you ... *(Of course she is, but she just can't confront him.)* I know you'll pay me back when you can. Didn't you put something in a Swiss account? I know they're boring, but they know how to store money.... Take that call. I'll talk to you soon. *(She hangs up the phone. She goes back to looking at the magazine article. She notices that her hands are shaking violently. The doorbell rings. Marina sits for a moment. Then she gets up and goes to open the door. Carol is standing there. Marina is very surprised.)*

CAROL. Hi.

MARINA. What on earth are you doing here?

CAROL. It doesn't make sense does it?

MARINA. I suppose you came to gloat over my misfortune.

CAROL. Not a bad place to start. *(Marina walks back to the couch and sits down. She continues going through her papers and pictures.)*

MARINA. Please come in.

CAROL. Should I make myself at home, or should I stand around awkwardly?

MARINA. I would much prefer the latter. *(Carol comes in and closes the door behind her. She is carrying her purse in one hand and the manila envelope under her arm. She leans against the closed door and regards Marina.)* Aren't you furious with me?

CAROL. I've never been madder at one human being. I wanted to deposit the check then forget about you and this whole stupid event.

MARINA. I'm flat broke. I have to move out of this apartment. I'm the laughingstock of the whole country.... Doesn't that make you feel somewhat better?

CAROL. Maybe a little.... But then I asked myself; feeding off the misfortune of some pathetic, miserable, spoiled piece of aging Swiss cheesecake.... What kind of a life is that? *(Marina takes a long look at Carol who is smiling angrily.)*

MARINA. So tell me, what kind of a life is it?

CAROL. Where are you going?

MARINA. I haven't decided yet. I might go back to Switzerland. I've been offered a job doing publicity at a hotel outside Lucerne.

CAROL. I thought you'd be a basket case over losing all that money.

MARINA. I've been poor and I've been rich. I'd rather be rich, but I know how to survive. *(Carol continues walking around. She can't help but be impressed by Marina's grit.)*

CAROL. Don't you feel really stupid about lending BT all your money?

MARINA. Not at all.

CAROL. Well you should. It was one of the all-time idiot plays of modern civilization.

MARINA. Don't forget; I got my man to marry me. Some women think so little of themselves, they can only get passionate about men who treat them like napkins.

CAROL. You can't say anything to me, I haven't said to my own mirror a hundred times. Are you as lonely as I am? *(Ma-*

rina is taken aback. She stops pouring over her papers and stares at Carol.)

MARINA. Look ... I did a terrible thing. I made you think we were friends because I was angry at you. Then I let you know we weren't ... I know you hate me ... I don't care one bit ...

CAROL. I only asked you if you were as lonely as I am?

MARINA. No!...

CAROL. I'm glad.

MARINA. Why would you be glad?... Why would you care one bit about me? Stop it, this instant.

CAROL. I didn't say I cared about you. I said I was glad you weren't as lonely as I am.... When Joe died, I lost the only friend I had.... And I don't have a clue in the world how to make one new friend.

MARINA. Go to the library. There must be a thousand books on how to make friends.

CAROL. Do you really think so?

MARINA. *(Pauses.)* No ...

CAROL. Why did you do that to me?

MARINA. You got well paid. What are you complaining about? Joe worked you over for twenty years and you have nothing to show for it. I manipulated you for a few weeks and you got a hundred thousand.... Be thankful. It's tough out there ...

CAROL. No, it's tough right here ...

MARINA. Carol, I have a heart of stone and the survival instincts of a wolf. Either be witty and make me laugh, or leave. *(Carol puts the manila envelope on a chair and walks over to Marina's pile of papers and photo albums.)*

CAROL. *(Casual.)* Are you still talking to BT?

MARINA. Of course.... I've known him for over twenty-five years. He's still my best friend.

CAROL. Really?... Isn't he spending night and day with Melody? Didn't he give her an engagement ring with a rock the size of a Honda? Doesn't he say Melody is the only woman he's ever been completely comfortable with?

MARINA. There is no connection between what BT says and

what he feels.

CAROL. If a man left me for another woman, first I would kill him, then I would never speak to him again.

MARINA. How can you say that? You wasted twenty years on a man who spent every night with another woman.

CAROL. That was our agreement. He didn't promise to be faithful and then lie to me.

MARINA. Twenty years, over seven thousand nights.

CAROL. I know how many nights it was. He never lied to me. I never had a "best friend" who took my fifty million dollars and lost it all.

MARINA. You should be so lucky. *(They stare angrily at each other. At the same time the absurdity and humor of the situation strikes them. They both turn away from each other so neither can see the other start to laugh. When they turn back to face each other, they both have sobered up at the same time.)*

CAROL. You know Joe almost spent a night with me. I was producing his show, and we were doing it out of California for a week. Joe said he wanted something unusual that would get attention. I scheduled this cute young comedian who wasn't that funny, but he showed me a gimmick I knew would get attention. The comedian comes on. He gets ninety seconds into his act and there isn't one laugh. Joe is looking offstage at me, really annoyed. Then the comedian takes the water glass off Joe's desk and smashes it on the floor. The guy gets down and begins to eat the glass off the floor. The audience is horrified. Joe is frozen, catatonic; there is a man in his studio on all fours eating glass. The guy looks up and says, "Gee Joe, I hope your floor is clean." The audience goes nuts laughing and applauding. The guy jumps up, takes a bow and disappears. I chase after him down the hall as he runs to an ambulance he had waiting. He stops and turns to me and says with little bubbles of blood popping out of his mouth "Thanks for the opportunity; they loved it." Joe was so upset that somebody would do that just to get on television. He came to my hotel room and talked for hours about the responsibility of people who work in television. He began to feel that he wasn't much different from the glass-eater. I never told Joe I knew in advance the guy was going to eat glass. I felt bad about it then. I feel worse about it now.... We held each other for a long time. He had just fallen asleep, when the phone rang. His wife in New York was having her appendix out. I drove him straight to the airport, and neither of us said a word. We never came close to spending a night together anywhere.

MARINA. What happened to the glass eater?

CAROL. He had a brief vogue for a few months. He took the money he made and invested in a computer software company. Last I heard, he was worth about a few million and lives in Colorado. He sends me a Christmas card every year.

MARINA. Does he still do comedy?

CAROL. *(Laughs in spite of herself. She can't stop laughing.)* Damnit, that was really funny.

MARINA. BT says I have no sense of humor.

CAROL. Your best friend says you have no sense of humor?

MARINA. Nothing will shake my confidence in BT. You are wasting your time.

CAROL. No I'm not. The sight of you in a sweat suit packing up the remains of your shattered life.... You have no idea how entertaining that is to me.... Just think, now you'll be able to go on a real date. You won't have to worry anymore if somebody is just after your money. *(She picks a few eight-by-ten photos off the coffee table and looks at them.)* You really looked good in tights. Where was this?

MARINA. That's BT and me at Aspen a few years ago.

CAROL. I'll bet you're a better skier than he is.

MARINA. Better skier, better tennis player, better golfer.

CAROL. He must've hated that.

MARINA. He loved it. I was a world-class athlete. If it hadn't have been for the accident, I would have at least two Olympic medals.

CAROL. Big deal; two more things to pack. *(She regards the photograph again. Finally.)* I don't have one picture of me with Joe. He was always afraid his wife would somehow find them ... *(She drops the picture back on the table. She sinks into a chair.)*

Twenty years. I deserved at least one picture.... Don't you think? *(She starts to cry. Marina regards her for a few seconds.)* I made the bargain. I knew what the deal was. But.... It would be so much easier if I had a picture ...

MARINA. Don't you want to forget him and get on with your life?

CAROL. Get on with what?... I don't have anybody to talk to. Who do I tell a joke to?... I'm going to be alone from now on. I live too far away from the median reality. Nobody's going to follow directions to get to me, all those twists, turns and half-painted signs ... *(Marina moves near to Carol. Marina is distressed to see her crying. Marina starts to reach out to touch her. Then Marina moves away.)*

MARINA. I'm sorry ...

CAROL. *(Cynical.)* I really believe that. Let me take a moment while I take your sympathy to my breast and comfort myself with your warm sincerity ...

MARINA. I deserve that.

CAROL. No, what you deserve is to be sent to live in the middle of Alaska, ten miles from the nearest restaurant, fifteen miles from the nearest store and fifty miles from the nearest person who understands the word "interior decorator." You *don't* deserve what you're getting.

MARINA. And what am I getting? *(Carol stands up. She walks to the table and picks the manila envelope up. She tosses it angrily to Marina who catches it deftly.)*

CAROL. That!... *(Carol exits out the front door without looking back. Marina opens the envelope and takes out a two inch thick manuscript.)*

MARINA. *(Reading the title page.) The Best of It* by Marina Cliff.... Oh no!... You wrote the book! *(She drops the manuscript on the floor as if it had burned her.)* How could you?... Why did you?... *(She paces around in real distress. She angrily kicks the manuscript across the floor. Then she goes and picks it up. She goes to the front door and opens it. She is about to throw the manuscript out. Yells out the door.)* You miserable wretch!... *(She can't resist opening to the first page. She starts to read and can't stop.)* Damn her.

Damn her to hell!... *(She closes the door. She goes to the couch and continues to read the manuscript. She starts to cry as the curtain comes down.)*

END OF SCENE 1

Scene 2

The lights come up to reveal that Carol is sitting at her downstage table. She is wearing a fashionable black pants suit. Her back is slightly to the audience as she talks on the phone. There is a drink on the table, but she is not stirring it with her finger.

CAROL. It's nice of you to pressure me like this, but I'm taking my time deciding. It's been so long since I've had options; I want to consider them awhile. I'm responding well to money ... *(She shifts toward the audience. Her jacket opens. We see she is wearing a bright red blouse. This is the first time we've seen her in anything other than black.)* Some people get a bit of money, and they go all to hell ... I've already been there. *(Laughs.)* I've got to go; I have a meeting. My new status has pried open some strange doors. *(She hangs up. She arranges herself and crosses her legs to reveal she is wearing bright green socks which clash terribly with the blouse. After a few seconds, Melody Charm walks in from R. She is an amazingly beautiful young woman who wears a cream-colored skirt-suit, beige blouse, pale lightly-patterned stockings and beige high-heeled shoes. She doesn't wear a watch or any jewelry except for an engagement ring with a diamond half as big as her thumb. The diamond reflects light like midday sun in a car mirror. She walks carefully over to Carol's table.)*

MELODY. Carol?

CAROL. *(Amused.)* Yes.

MELODY. I'm Melody Charm.

CAROL. Hi, Myrna. Sit down. *(Melody sits down at the table. She is very careful how she crosses her legs.)*

MELODY. That's so sweet. Nobody has called me "Myrna" in such a long time.
CAROL. Me neither.
MELODY. Ha.... Ha ... *(Her laugh is very controlled and sounds exactly like it's written.)* This is a charming little unrealized place. *(She is trying to sound sophisticated.)*
CAROL. Yes, it has a certain inevitable insouciance.
MELODY. Ha ... Ha ... *(She carefully adjusts the neck on her sweater.)* I appreciate you taking the time to meet me. I'm a bit nervous. I don't often meet people alone anymore.
CAROL. It can be traumatic.... Would you like a drink?
MELODY. No thank you. I don't drink before midnight.
CAROL. Really? Would you mind telling me about that?
MELODY. Yes ... *(Carol stares at Melody who stares back with a dazzling smile.)* BT says I should always get right to the point; I want to be a journalist. BT thinks you might be able to help me. He says you're a very creative person.
CAROL. Did he say what I've "created"?
MELODY. No.... We don't tend to have detailed discussions on the arts.
CAROL. That's probably in the best interests of us all.
MELODY. Ha.... Ha ...
CAROL. What would you like to know about writing?
MELODY. What does a writer do exactly?
CAROL. Everybody's been wondering that for about a thousand years.
MELODY. BT doesn't like it when I talk to journalists. I wonder why he wants me to be one.
CAROL. If you were interviewing him, that would be a good question to ask.
MELODY. No it wouldn't ... *(Carol stares at her. Again Melody smiles and goes right on.)* Suppose you were interviewing me. What kind of questions would you ask?
CAROL. That depends; am I being a reporter or am I a creative writer doing a profile?
MELODY. What's the difference? What kind of questions would a reporter ask me?
CAROL. Where were you born? How many beauty contests

have you entered? What's your shoe size?

MELODY. And if you were a writer?

CAROL. When did you lose your virginity? What the hell do you do all day? What kind of prenuptial agreement do you have? Doesn't it hurt your feelings to be called a "bimbo" or a "decoration"?

MELODY. *(After a pause.)* Wouldn't it hurt your feelings?

CAROL. I'd love to be called a bimbo. It would make me so happy.

MELODY. *(After a pause.)* I have agreed not to take one penny if we split up.

CAROL. But you get to keep the ring and all the other jewelry he's given you.

MELODY. I give it all back. Those are like crown jewels; they go with the position.

CAROL. Which position is that?

MELODY. Ha.... Ha ...

CAROL. Don't you get lonely?

MELODY. *(Hesitates. Then makes a joke.)* I always have my hair to keep me company.

CAROL. Ha.... Ha ... *(Melody starts to giggle. She forces herself to stop.)* Do you know his ex-wife, Marina?

MELODY. We haven't met. BT says it would be confusing. They're still good friends. He depends on her a lot.

CAROL. Does he tell you about all those little habits of hers that he once loved but now he finds annoying? Does he tell you about those little habits of yours that he now loves and will cherish forever?

MELODY. Yes. Marina used to understand him so well.

CAROL. Until she suddenly "changed." She woke up one morning and seemed suddenly not to know how wonderful and exciting he was.

MELODY. Yes.... How did you know?

CAROL. I don't know how I do it. *(Melody senses something is amiss, but she has good animal instincts.)*

MELODY. This isn't going like it's supposed to.

CAROL. Just like life.

MELODY. You seem sad.

CAROL. *(Taken aback. She recovers quickly.)* No, if you want to be a reporter, you take a much more predatory approach. You would say to me, "How long have you been sad?

MELODY. How long has it been?

CAROL. *(Angry, but covers it up. With grudging admiration.)* I'm not sure I can teach you anything.

MELODY. That's what BT says to me all the time.

CAROL. *(After a moment.)* Damn, people are interesting. I have to get out more. *(Melody stands up.)*

MELODY. You know Marina don't you?

CAROL. Slightly.

MELODY. She wrote a novel you know. It's just out today. The bookstore next door has a window full of them. *The Best of It* it's called. It's gotten some great reviews. Are you going to read it?

CAROL. No ...

MELODY. I enjoyed this ...

CAROL. You didn't learn too much about writing.

MELODY. It's probably all for the best. *(She heads toward R.)* BT has me on a very tight schedule. I must be going. *(They shake hands.)*

CAROL. Yes. You don't want to be late for your sexual harassment seminar. *(She regrets having said this the moment it is out of her mouth. Melody simply tilts her head to one side and regards Carol quizzically for a beat. Melody walks off R. Carol sits there for a moment.*

Marina walks on from L. She wears a simple skirt and blouse under an old raincoat. She is carrying an armful of newspapers and magazines. She angrily bangs a magazine down on the table.)

MARINA. *New York Times Review of Books:* "Marina Cliff has written a poignant, revealing, skillful first novel." *(She bangs a magazine on the table.) New York Magazine:* "*The Best of It* by Marina Cliff is a compelling, powerful first novel." *(She bangs another magazine on the table.) The New Yorker:* "I laughed and I cried. Marina Cliff has given us a novel for today and for the ages." *(She glares at Carol.)*

CAROL. *(Calmly.)* Congratulations.

MARINA. You bitch. You incredible, mean, horrible, creature. You wrote a great book. Damnit to hell, *I* couldn't put it down. Everybody is calling me from all over the world, interviews, talk shows, publishers offering me millions for my next book!...

CAROL. Technically, they're offering *me* millions for your next book.

MARINA. Why couldn't you just write a simple trash novel? You betrayed me!...

CAROL. I betrayed us both.... Feel better?

MARINA. What am I going to do? I can't talk to people about this book. I certainly can't write another.

CAROL. Neither can I.

MARINA. *(She sits down.)* How could you do that? You wrote the story of you and Joe with such passion and ... and *life*.... You lied a little here and there.

CAROL. I enjoyed that part of it.

MARINA. Don't just sit there. This isn't what we talked about. You have to tell me what to say in interviews. If it gets out that I didn't write it, I'll be the joke of the world.

CAROL. For about ten minutes ... *(She picks up the top magazine and looks at it.)*

MARINA. Carol!... *(She yanks the magazine away from Carol.)* Listen to me!...

CAROL. What for?... Our relationship is over ...

MARINA. No it isn't!... You know what really kills me about the book. I can tell how good it felt to write it, to do something that great. It was like the six months before my ligament was destroyed; I was skating *great*. I don't have anything like that. I can't do anything great ... I hate it!...

CAROL. Tell me about the ligament, Marina.

MARINA. *(She stops cold.)* I told you. I told you the whole story.

CAROL. Yes, you told me the story ... *(They stare at each other. Marina is in a rage. Carol just smiles. Melody comes walking on from R. Carol sees her first. Marina turns around. They both watch as Melody walks to the table and sits down carefully. She takes Carol's drink and empties the glass in one gulp. She looks at Carol and then at Marina.)*

MELODY. You'll never guess what happened.
CAROL. The warranty expired on your Wonderbra.
MELODY. Ha.... Ha ... *(Suddenly Marina grabs Melody's left hand.)*
MARINA. *(In a rage.)* The ring.... Where's the ring?... Where the hell is the damn ring?
MELODY. In a limo on it's way back ...
MARINA. It's over?
MELODY. It's over ...
CAROL. It's over?
MARINA. Why?... What happened? What did you do?
MELODY. I don't know. I called him to check on where we were meeting this evening. He said it was over. He wanted the ring back. He hung up. That was it. *(She starts to cry.)*
MARINA. He doesn't mean it. He does this all the time. He forgot to drink water or take his B-twelve shot ...
MELODY. He's never done it to me.
MARINA. I'll straighten this out. *(She grabs the phone and punches up the number with her left hand. She offers her right to Melody.)* I'm Marina ...
MELODY. *(Shaking the hand.)* Melody Charm.... Pleased to meet you.
MARINA. *(Into phone.)* Sally, get me BT right now. I don't care who he's talking to ... I said interrupt him. Tell him it's Joyful Judy ...
CAROL. Joyful Judy?...
MARINA. He'll be on the phone in less than ... *(Into phone.)* BT, how are you?... Yes, I'm thrilled about the book. Have you been getting your B-twelve shots?... What's going on then? Why did you tell Melody it's over?... Never mind how I knew so fast. Why?... *(She listens.)* Did you ask her if it was true?... You idiot.... You are an idiot ... *(She looks at the phone.)* He hung up on me ... *(She calmly puts the phone back in it's cradle.)*
CAROL. Did he ask her what?
MARINA. He says he broke it off because you told somebody what BT really means ...
CAROL. It means "Big Thing" ...
MARINA. *(To Melody.)* Did you?

MELODY. Yes ...
MARINA. *You're* the idiot. You know the rules.
MELODY. Are the rules more important than me?
MARINA. Are you a bimbo or not?
MELODY. I thought I was. Now I'm confused.
CAROL. What the hell does BT really mean?
MELODY. "Big Thing" ...
MARINA. Of course it means "Big Thing".... But when I first called him that twenty years ago, he weighed two hundred and thirty pounds. I was talking about him.. He was a big guy. He thought I meant something else ... I never corrected him, because you don't ...
MELODY. You don't do that with a man ...
MARINA. He loved the nickname. The press loved it, and it was great for business ...
CAROL. Hold it, hold it, hold it!... Are you telling me, this guy broke off an engagement over ... over *that?*
MARINA. He can be very sensitive ...
CAROL. Sensitive?.. Girls, the reality boat sailed and you missed it.
MARINA. There's no need to be nasty.
CAROL. There's a desperate need.
MELODY. *(Starts to cry again.)* What do I do? Every reporter in the world is going to ask me what happened.
CAROL. Confuse and disorient everybody: tell the truth ...
MARINA. No!... This is a man with serious pride ... I beg you, don't underestimate him ... *(Melody stands up slowly.)* What are you going to do?
MELODY. I'll get him back. I'm not totally without resources. *(She stretches her perfect torso like a cat. She moves her hips sensually. Carol and Marina stare in envy at this perfect body in motion.)* When I sit around, I get stiff.
MARINA. So does everybody else I imagine.
MELODY. Thank you both so much for the advice. *(She walks across and exits R. Carol and Marina sit there in a daze.)*
CAROL. *(Finally.)* I don't hate her because she has skin like a prom queen. I don't hate her because she has perfect hair that obeys every command. I don't even hate her because

when she enters a room full of men the testosterone level rises like steam from a swamp.

MARINA. You hate her because of how much time she has. *(Carol regards Marina. Carol holds up her open hand. Marina slaps it in a high five.)*

CAROL and MARINA. Ha.... Ha.... *(The two women regard each other fondly.)*

CAROL. *(Finally.)* Here's your window of opportunity.

MARINA. Go back to him?

CAROL. Wasn't that the first thing that crossed your mind?

MARINA. Sure it was, but so what? The first thing that crossed my mind when I read your book was to murder you, but I'm not going to do that either.

CAROL. *Your* book.

MARINA. Doesn't it kill you to have written such a beautiful story about you and Joe, and your name isn't on it?

CAROL. I'm like an old watch that got taken apart and put back together with a few pieces missing inside. I look okay, and I run most of the time, but I won't last.

MARINA. Talk to me.

CAROL. I like the raincoat.

MARINA. Carol!... I'm so.... Look, I know I was an impossible spoiled bitch, but I'm changing. We can be great friends ...

CAROL. My friends tell me the truth.

MARINA. I'll tell you the truth. I'll tell you about BT. This is something nobody in the world knows but me; he irons his money.... He gets up in the middle of the night and goes to the laundry room with a stack of bills ...

CAROL. Marina ...

MARINA. Also, he's afraid of naked feet.

CAROL. Tell me about your skating accident.

MARINA. *(Angry.)* Why do you keep asking about that?

CAROL. I don't keep asking about it. This is the second time.

MARINA. It was a very painful time in my life. I had worked every day for most of my life toward one goal. When that girl skated into me and cut my ligament, it was all over in an instant. I can't bear to think about it. *(Marina looks defiantly at*

Carol. Carol abruptly changes tack.)

CAROL. *(Soothing.)* I understand. It must have been just terrible ...

MARINA. *(She is uneasy with Carol's penetrating and ever-so-slightly mocking air.)* It was.

CAROL. Tell me about Joyful Judy.

MARINA. No!...

CAROL. Okay. I knew you wouldn't tell me anything really important anyway ...

MARINA. *(After a pause.)* Okay.... Joyful Judy was the name of an actress in a porno film we saw twenty-some years ago in London. BT was very shy about asking for what he wanted.... Over the years, if he wanted to be intimate, he would call me Judy. If he wanted something exotic he would call me Joyful Judy. After we broke up, he would sometimes call me up and ask for "Judy" ...

CAROL. *(Hesitates.)* Joe would call me "Punch" ... *(She shrugs.)* It was what my father called me when I was little. I was always ready to do battle. I told Joe about it and he got a big kick out of the name. One time he sent me a pornographic cartoon where the girl was named Punch. From then on it was a code word. Once in the middle of a fight, he tried to smooth things over by saying "Punch." I hit him right in the face.... He loved it ... *(Carol laughs. Marina laughs with her.)* I miss him ... I miss him so much. He could be such a jerk, but he knew from our first contact I was a real person with feelings. Most people you meet, think you're just an actor in their play.

MARINA. That's so true; if you don't pick up the right cues they recast you.

CAROL. *(She laughs with genuine appreciation.)* Oh God, that is perfect ...

MARINA. *(Pleased.)* In the beginning, BT knew I was a real person. I loved those early days when we were out to conquer the world together. Later on I was just.... It was so damn lonely. It was worse than if I'd never had anybody. Why would that be?

CAROL. I know it's true, but I don't know why.

MARINA. I had an affair with BT's right hand man and he has no idea it happened ...

CAROL. Are you kidding?

MARINA. No. It was about ten years ago. I went to BT's office. He had forgotten about our lunch date for the thousandth time. His number two guy, Steve Jensen, was interviewing new secretaries in his office next door. I went out, got a wig, glasses, a simple dress and went back. About an hour later, they told me to go in and meet Steve. He didn't recognize me at all.... When the interview was over he stood up to shake my hand. I ran a finger up the back of his wrist. He pulled me to him.... We tore each other to pieces. It was fantastic. I thanked him politely and left ...

CAROL. Must've been a great wig.

MARINA. *(Chuckles.)* I've never told anybody about that. He died of a heart attack two years ago. I was really sad.

CAROL. What about the accent?

MARINA. *(Wary.)* What?

CAROL. The accent.... Your European accent is very distinctive. Why didn't he recognize it?

MARINA. *(Hesitates.)* I don't need the accent. *(She says this in perfect English without a trace of the accent. From now to the end, Marina talks with a normal American accent.)*

CAROL. *(Truly stunned. She has to take a moment. Finally she says admiringly.)* Oh you devil. You incredible devil.

MARINA. How about that?

CAROL. I can't believe it.... Why?... *(She realizes.)* BT liked the accent.

MARINA. He loved it.... It turned him on. He still doesn't know. Willy, my skating coach, was from Wisconsin. I learned a perfect American accent by listening to him. You're the only one who knows.

CAROL. You are an amazing woman.... Damn it to hell, I wish we could be ...

MARINA. Maybe we can.

CAROL. Let's stop this right here.

MARINA. Don't underestimate either one of us.

CAROL. Why not? I do it so well. *(The two women regard*

each other. Finally Marina picks up the phone and punches up a number.)

MARINA. *(Into phone with her accent.)* Martha, this is Marina Cliff calling. Let me speak to Barbara.... You sound strange are you okay?... You've been reading my book and you can't stop crying?... *(She gives Carol a look.)* Thank you so much.... Barbara's in Japan?. Okay, I'll call somebody else. *(She hangs up and as she dials another number, she says to Carol without the accent.)* She says she's in Japan ... I know that means she's having another facelift. *(Into phone with the accent.)* Hello, this is Marina Cliff calling. May I speak to Diane ... Diane, how've you been? It was delightful to see you and Mike at The MOMA last week. Oh you're right, it was at The BAM.... Thank you, it's quite a thrill. Listen would you do me a huge favor. Would you interview me for just a few minutes on your show this week?... I think you'll be interested in this. The book I wrote that everybody is going crazy about.... I didn't write it. It was written by a woman named Carol Spearman.... No, I'll tell you all about it on the show.... The new hair is sensational by the way.... Bye.... *(Marina hangs up the phone. She stands up and walks off L. She says without the accent.)* Have fun.... *(Marina exits. Carol sits there for a long moment. She picks up one of the magazines and begins to read the review of her book as the curtain comes down.)*

END OF SCENE 2

Scene 3

The curtain comes up on Marina's apartment. The furniture has been moved around. The pictures are gone from the walls, and the kinetic sculpture is gone. The nymph lamps have been replaced by simple department store lamps. However, the pink and green ceramic dog is still in the same place. There are several cartons of books on the floor. The phone rings. After the third ring, the front door opens and Carol backs in carrying another carton of books. She is wearing jeans and a simple cashmere sweater. She has on athletic socks but no shoes.

CAROL. I'm here, don't hang up!... *(She walks into the room and deposits the carton of books on the floor next to the other boxes. The phone continues to ring. She takes out a book and regards it for a moment. The phone stops ringing.)*

I said, don't hang up. *(She goes back to looking at the book. The phone starts ringing again. She grabs a portable phone off the coffee table. As if she were an answering machine.)*

Hello, this is Carol.... I'm here and listening to your call. Start talking and I'll decide within thirty seconds if I want to deal with you right now.... *(She listens.)* David.... How are you?... I'm so glad to hear it. When you didn't call last week, I assumed you'd been taken hostage.... *(She goes out the other door as she continues talking.)*

That was a joke, David.... *(She disappears out the door. After a moment, she comes back holding a dog food dish with something in it.)*

No, thank you. I don't go to the opera unless it says I have to on the ransom note.... *(As she listens, she crosses and puts the dog dish down in front of the ceramic dog. She pats the dog fondly.)*

Now, be a good boy.... Not you David. I was talking to my dog.... No, not tomorrow. Anyway, I find eating lunch in museums non life-affirming.... What made you decide to call me just now? Are you at the doctor's waiting for the results of your annual spine-search? Yes, I thought we hit it off well too, but you didn't call me for a week, and you have no idea what I'm talking about ninety percent of the time. *(She holds the phone away from her and screams silently. Then she puts the phone back to her ear.)*

David, not only do I not want you to call me again. I don't want you to call any woman ever again.... *(She clicks off the phone and tosses it on the couch. There is a knock at the front door. Carol quickly exits through the other door. There is another knock. Then a key is inserted in the door. Marina walks in. She pockets her key and closes the door behind her. Marina is wearing a plain skirt and sweater with simple black shoes. She is carrying a package under her arm about eight by ten inches and two inches thick. She stands by the door. Carol comes back into the room. She is wearing a beautiful blue suit, but the blouse doesn't match and it isn't tucked in. She is wearing pantyhose and green shoes that look terrible. She looks over at Marina.)*

MARINA. You should change the lock.

CAROL. That's on my list right after "save the ozone layer."

MARINA. Mind if I come in?

CAROL. Please, make yourself uncomfortable.... How do you like my place?

MARINA. It's aggressively grotesque.

CAROL. I had help, but the concept was all mine. *(Marina walks into the room. She puts the package on the arm of the couch. She sees the ceramic dog with the food in front of it.)*

MARINA. *(Smiles.)* What's he eating?

CAROL. He's not. He won't touch it.

MARINA. Why did you move into my old apartment?

CAROL. It was vacant. Not quite as vacant as when you lived here, but....

MARINA. I came by to make sure you're okay. You haven't been seen lately.... I'm staying in the Fogarty's triplex down the street while they cruise.

CAROL. I'm glad you found a comfortable place.

MARINA. I didn't say that.... I found something wonderful to do. I'm working with the Olympic Committee, counseling young athletes on how to balance their lives. It's difficult sometimes, but I know I can help. *(She walks over to the couch.)* BT and Melody got married this morning.

CAROL. The bimbo and the billionaire. I didn't choose to attend the nuptials.... According to CNN they winged off to a private island hideaway.

MARINA. I also chose not to attend. How do you like being a celebrity?

CAROL. It's an affliction for which there may be no cure.

MARINA. The book continues to sell very well.

CAROL. Yes. They expect the paperback and movie rights to bring God knows how much.

MARINA. Are you dating anyone?

CAROL. A couple of scuds flew over, but I was never in any danger.

MARINA. *(Laughs.)* I know what you mean.... I didn't think he'd get married again.

CAROL. I did. He needs to take title to something before he can renovate it.

MARINA. How can you understand someone so well when you've never met them?

CAROL. What I don't understand is why you came to see me.

MARINA. You really don't? *(Carol says nothing. Marina looks Carol over.)* Those shoes.... Give them to me.... *(Carol takes the shoes off and hands them to Marina. Marina takes the shoes and walks quickly through the other door. Carol sits there like a little girl. A few seconds later, Marina comes out carrying a beige blouse. She holds it out to Carol.)* Go put this on. Don't you have anything but slippers and sneakers?

CAROL. I don't know.

MARINA. Go.... Put it on. I'll think of something. *(Carol obeys and goes through the other door. Marina looks around the room.)* Did you ever get together with Melody again?

CAROL. *(Offstage.)* She came to interview me awhile back. It didn't go very well. She was still broken up with BT.

MARINA. You mean when she was working for that magazine. It was a joke. They never published one of her interviews.

CAROL. *(Offstage.)* She was pretty scared when she came to see me.

MARINA. Poor thing. *(Carol comes back out. She is buttoning the beige blouse. Marina walks over to her and tucks the blouse in. She adjusts Carol's jacket and fluffs up her hair.)* That's much better....

CAROL. Melody told me when they were supposedly hating each other, BT went to her apartment one night and attacked her. *(Marina stands still and stares at Carol.)* Doesn't that horrify you?

MARINA. Yes it does.... But the worst thing is, I'm thinking, "Why didn't he ever attack me?" What's wrong with me?... I wish he'd made the attempt. Do you understand?

CAROL. Of course....

MARINA. How can you have no shoes? *(Carol simply looks at Marina.)* Sit down.... *(She takes off her shoes and puts them on Carol.)*

CAROL. What's happened with the money?

MARINA. He'll pay it back.

CAROL. No he won't. Not unless you embarrass him about it.

MARINA. I don't want to talk about it.

CAROL. Aren't you terrified?

MARINA. *(Lying.)* No. *(She regards Carol.)* Stand up.... *(Carol stands up. She looks pretty good.)* That's the best I can do right now. I'll see you around. *(She heads for the door. Carol stands there fighting back tears.)*

CAROL. Marina, you forgot your package.

MARINA. That's for you.... *(She exits out the front door. Carol goes to the package and picks it up. She tears the paper off it and opens it up. It is a frame with a picture in it. Carol looks at it and begins to cry. Then she runs to the door and yells.)*

CAROL. Marina!... Marina!... Come back please!... *(There is no sound. Carol walks back to the couch and leans against it. She looks at the picture. Marina silently comes in the door and leans against the wall the same way Carol did when she first came to the apartment.)*

MARINA. Yes...?

CAROL. This picture of me and Joe. Where did you get it?

MARINA. I had a friend of mine at the network search all the archives. It took her a month, but she found it. Did you read the inscription?

CAROL. No.... *(She looks at the picture and reads.)* "To Punch with love from her friend Judy" *(She is still for a moment. Then she stamps her foot like a little girl and yells angrily.)* Why did you do that?... Why?.. Leave me alone!... Go away!...

MARINA. Carol, I'm your friend....

CAROL. How do I know that? *(Marina gets up and puts her*

hands on Carol's shoulders.)

MARINA. Carol.... Tell me....

CAROL. *(After a beat.)* I told you I never had any friends. Well, when I was eight I had one friend. Elaine Bragdon. Everybody called her "Cherry." She was the most prettiest most popular girl in the fourth grade. She thought I was funny and tough. We went everywhere together, to the movies, swimming. One day she heard my father call me "Punch." He was dying, but none of us knew it. From then on that was all Cherry called me. She and Joe and my father are the only ones who ever called me that.... *(She stops for a second.)* One afternoon we were walking to her house when this kid, Tony, began bothering her. She ignored him. Suddenly he pushed her down on the sidewalk. I went crazy, yelling and screaming at him.... He ran crying down the street. When I helped Cherry up, I could see she was afraid of me not Tony.... The next day at school, she was polite and distant. I got so mad. I began yelling at her that we were best friends, that she loved me and I loved her.... She turned and walked away down the hall, her little white shoes squeaking. She never talked to me again....

MARINA. I'll kill her.... *(Carol tries to laugh through the tears.)*

CAROL. *(Hugging the picture.)* This picture means to much to me.... Marina I....

MARINA. *(Gently cuts her off.)* When that girl skated into me, and I went down on the ice. I knew I was okay. It hurt, but it was only a small cut and a bruise. Willy carried me to the locker room and went to call the doctor. I told the other girls I wanted to be alone.... I took off my skate and jabbed the blade into the side of my knee as hard as I could. I could feel the ligament let go.... Oh God help me, it was such a relief. It was such a relief.... *(She slides down the wall as she bursts into tears. Carol walks over to Marina and sits down beside her. Carol also cries as she holds the sobbing Marina. After a time, the phone rings. Carol holds Marina and lets it ring.)* Please answer it. I left your number.

CAROL. It's not important.

MARINA. Please.... *(Carol gets up and goes to get the portable phone.)*

CAROL. Hello?... Yes she's right here.... *(She takes the phone over to Marina and hands it to her.)*

MARINA. BT.... Congratulations to you both.... The accent? I woke up one day, and it was gone. *(She smiles at Carol.)* Don't worry, I'm sure it's just one of your allergies.... Take one of the green capsules.... It sounds beautiful.... She's such a nice girl I.... *(Carol yanks the phone out of Marina's hand.)*

CAROL. *(Into phone.)* Richard, this is Carol Spearman. I'm just fine thank you. Tell me one thing; when are you going to give Marina back her money?... How much money do you have right now?...

MARINA. No.... No!... Don't do that!... He'll come after you.... He might kill you!...

CAROL. *(Waving Marina away.)* Don't you think Marina deserves at least half of that?... No, I will not let you talk to her.... Listen to me ....

MARINA. Carol, please ... *(Carol turns and looks at Marina. After a beat, Marina smiles and gives Carol a thumbs up.)* Go get him, Punch....

CAROL. *(Laughs and says into the phone.)* Don't interrupt me you infantile idiot.... You arrange for her to get a certified check by six o'clock tonight.... Why am I mad? You manipulated her, you humiliated her. You stole her money; you traded unfairly on her kindness and decency. Didn't I tell you not to interrupt me you rodent!... *(Screams.)* No, you listen to me. You give her that money, or I will kill you.... Oh please, send around some goons. I can't wait!... You have no idea what tough is. *(She grins and turns to Marina. Carol says back into the phone.)* Don't tell me your problems. If she doesn't have the money by the end of today, you're on a garbage scow to hell.... *(She takes a deep breath and points thumbs up to Marina.)* That sounds just fine, Richard. I know you'll enjoy your honeymoon so much more after you've done this little thing.... Six o'clock today. Send it to her old apartment. We'll be waiting.... Sure I'll tell you why I'm doing this. I'm her friend.... *(She hangs up. Marina stands up slowly. They look at each other.)*

MARINA. You think he'll send it?

CAROL. Who the hell knows?

MARINA. Who the hell cares? *(After a pause.)* You want to go to a movie or something?

CAROL. Sure. *(The two of them look at each other and begin to laugh. Carol looks down at Marina's stockinged feet.)* Were you really going to walk out in the street with no shoes on?

MARINA. What do you think?

CAROL. I think you took a big chance on me.

MARINA. Carol, did anybody ever tell you, you are the world's biggest softest marshmallow?

CAROL. I thought that was you. *(The laughter joins with tears as the two women hug.)*

MARINA. I love you, Punch....

CAROL. I love you Judy. *(The curtain comes down.)*

THE END

PROPERTY LIST

ACT ONE

PRESET

ON CAROL'S BAR TABLE

Black phone
Silverware
Glass with Pernod (green-yellow Gatorade)
Pink napkin
Flamingo swizzle stick

ON CHAIR TO CAROL'S LEFT

Briefcase with:
folder with pile of outlines
leather notepad
prescription bag with prescription with Tic Tacs

MARINA'S COFFEE TABLE

Tape for her recorder
Appointment book
Two picture frames

STAGE RIGHT PROP TABLE

Tape recorder
Purse Marina uses for Act One and Two
Dish of dog food for Carol—Act Two, Scene 3
3 magazines (book reviews) for Marina
Bottle of Evian water

STAGE LEFT PROP TABLE

Crossword puzzle with Mont Blanc pen on it for Carol to carry on
Envelope with check in it for stagehand to deliver to door Act One, Scene 3

Small packing carton for Carol to bring in
Tiffany bag with picture in frame in it for Marina
Carol's white portable phone for Act Two, Scene 2
3 glasses and green Gatorade (Carol's Pernod)

ACT TWO

PRESET

ON CAROL'S BAR TABLE
Manuscript in envelope on chair
Fresh drink etc., as in Act One, Scene 1

MARINA'S APARTMENT
One moving box to the L. of coffee table with new newspapers sticking out of it
Make sure appointment book, tape recorder, purse and coat are struck
2 picture frames lying flat on coffee table
5 books on couch, floor or side table

STAGE LEFT PROP TABLE
Briefcase, crossword puzzle with pen on top
Carol's clothes stacked:
jeans on bottom
purple sweater
green socks
black jacket

COSTUME PLOT

ACT ONE

Scene 1

MARINA
Cream-colored skirt-suit
Gold blouse
Light beige stockings
Cream-colored shoes
Lots of gold jewelry

CAROL
Black pants
Black shirt or sweater
Black shoes
Black socks

Scene 2

MARINA
Skintight stretch leopard suit with cream-colored Armani jacket
Matching high heels (the outfit should be over the top outrageous and get a laugh when Marina walks onstage)

CAROL
Same as Scene 1

Scene 3

MARINA
Light beige skirt
Gold blouse

Wide gold fabric belt
Cream-colored shoes
Stylish sand-colored jacket

CAROL
Same as Scene 1

Scene 1

MARINA
Blue or gray sweatsuit
Running shoes (no jewelry)

CAROL
Same as in Act One

Scene 2

MARINA
Simple skirt and blouse
Raincoat
Flat shoes
Large purse

CAROL
Black expensive pants suit
Bright red blouse, bright green socks
Black shoes

MELODY
Cream-colored skirt-suit
Beige blouse
Pale lightly-patterned stockings
Beige high-heeled shoes (skirt should be noticeably shorter than Marina's)

Scene 3

MARINA

Simple skirt and sweater
Plain black shoes

CAROL

Jeans
Nice sweater
Running shoes
Cream-colored chiffon skirt
Cream-colored harlequin blouse

SOUND EFFECTS

Telephone ring
Doorbell chimes

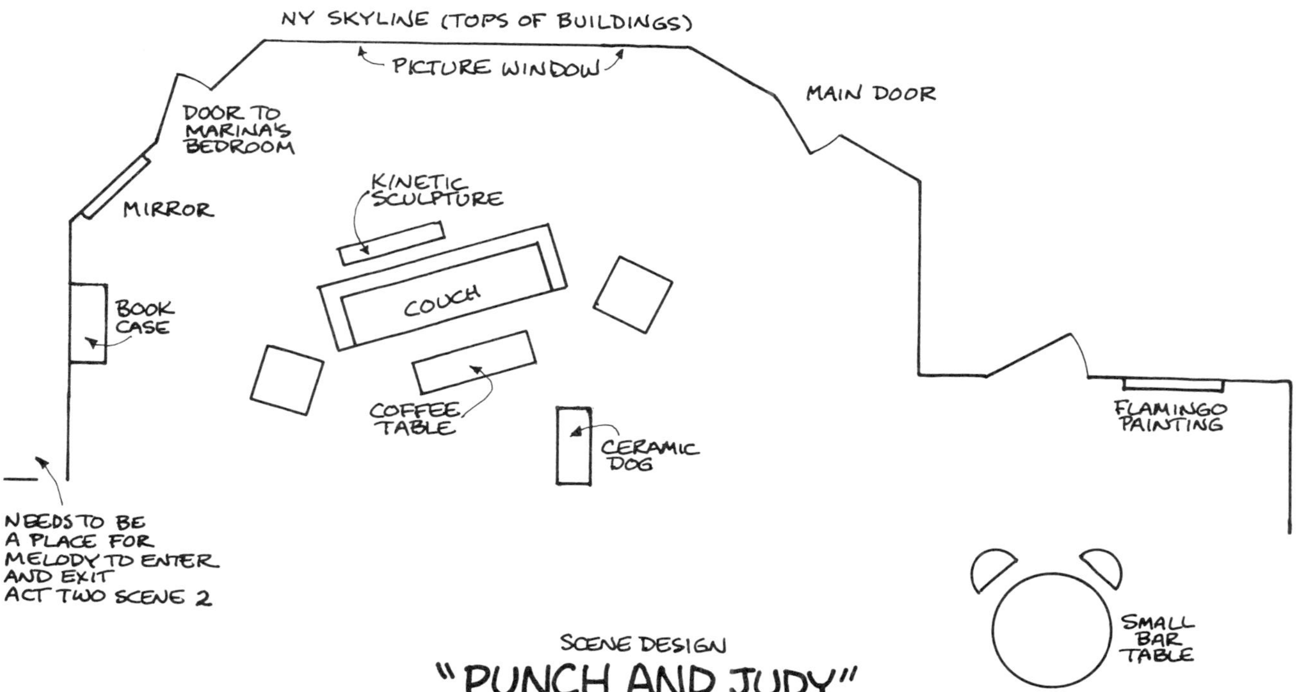

SCENE DESIGN

"PUNCH AND JUDY"

(DESIGNED BY COLEMAN MOSS FOR BURBAGE THEATRE)